Elements in Our Universe

by Beth Parlikar

Vocabulary

astronomer

characteristics

elements

fusion

metallic

properties

radiation

Word count: 2,755

Elements in
Our Universe

by Beth Parlikar

PEARSON

Scott
Foresman

Editorial Offices: Glenview, Illinois • Parsippany, New Jersey • New York, New York
Sales Offices: Needham, Massachusetts • Duluth, Georgia • Glenview, Illinois
Coppell, Texas • Ontario, California • Mesa, Arizona

Every effort has been made to secure permission and provide appropriate credit for photographic material. The publisher deeply regrets any omission and pledges to correct errors called to its attention in subsequent editions.

Unless otherwise acknowledged, all photographs are the property of Scott Foresman, a division of Pearson Education.

Photo locators denoted as follows: Top (T), Center (C), Bottom (B), Left (L), Right (R), Background (Bkgd)

Opener: ©DK Images; 1 ©DK Images; 3 Getty Images; 4 ©DK Images; 5 PhotoEdit; 6 PhotoEdit; 7 NASA; 8 PhotoEdit; 9 ©DK Images; 10 ©DK Images; 11 ©DK Images; 12 ©DK Images; 13 ©DK Images; 15 ©DK Images; 16 PhotoLibrary, Comstock, ©DK Images; 17 ©DK Images; 18 Fundamental; 19 Aurora Photos; 20 ©DK Images, Getty Images; 21 NASA; 23 ©DK Images

ISBN: 0-328-13609-3

7 8 9 10 V0G1 14 13 12 11 10 09 08

Matter Is Everywhere

Everything that we can see, taste, smell, or touch is made of matter. However, some things that cannot be seen, such as the air we breathe, are made of matter as well. Everything in your classroom is made of matter. Everything on Earth and even every substance in the universe is made of matter.

Where does matter come from? What are the different forms of matter? How do they change and interact? How do these changes and interactions affect life as we know it? You will find the answers to these questions in the following pages. Let's explore how matter makes up everything around us.

Elements and Compounds

Scientists have learned from experiments that matter is made of tiny particles that are far too small to see, even with powerful microscopes. These particles are called atoms, which comes from the ancient Greek word *atomos*, meaning "indivisible." The ancient Greeks believed that atoms were the smallest particles in existence and that they could not be divided into smaller parts. What scientists understand about atoms has changed a lot since the ancient Greeks first began hypothesizing about them.

Today, scientists know that atoms can be divided into smaller parts. They are made up of tinier particles called protons, neutrons, and electrons. Protons and neutrons clump together at the center of an atom to form what is called the nucleus. Electrons move quickly around the area outside the nucleus.

Oxygen

A molecule of water is made of one oxygen atom and two hydrogen atoms.

Hydrogen

Different kinds of atoms have different numbers of protons and electrons. The number of electrons and protons determines what kind of atom they are. For instance, helium, hydrogen, and iron atoms all have different numbers of protons and electrons. These basic substances are also called **elements.** Elements are substances with only one kind of atom. The atoms in an element will all be identical.

Some things are made from a single element, such as the copper that makes up copper wire. But most things are made from combinations of elements, such as water and air.

Atoms can bond together to form molecules, which are particles composed of two or more atoms. For example, a water molecule consists of one atom of oxygen bonded to two atoms of hydrogen: H_2O. In carbon dioxide, gas present in air, two oxygen atoms and one carbon atom are bonded together: CO_2.

Carbon and oxygen are both elements. When atoms of these two elements bond together to form molecules of the compound carbon dioxide, the characteristic qualities of each element change. Molecules of carbon dioxide mix with molecules of other compounds to form air. Air is a mixture. The molecules of a mixture are not bonded together; they are mixed, like the ingredients of a salad.

Pure iron is attracted to magnets.

Iron that has been mixed with sulfur and heated becomes ferrous sulfide, which is not attracted to magnets.

Amazing changes can happen when atoms of different elements combine. When two or more elements combine, the resulting product is called a compound. The traits of a compound are not always the same as those of the elements that make it up. The color, magnetism, state of matter, or other traits of the compound may be different from those of its individual elements.

Table salt, or sodium chloride, is a very common substance that is found all over the world. It is present in many rocks in Earth's crust as well as in ocean water. It is made from the elements sodium and chlorine. In their pure forms, sodium is a metal that reacts violently with water, and chlorine is a poisonous greenish-yellow gas. But when the two combine, table salt is formed. This harmless substance is different from both of these elements. It is a clear solid that does not react with water and is safe to eat.

Ferrous sulfide is another example of a compound that is different from the elements that are present in it. The element iron is a hard, shiny, gray metal that is attracted to magnets. Sulfur is a soft, yellow powder with a strong smell. It is not attracted to magnets. When heated and mixed, the iron and sulfur form ferrous sulfide. This is a dark gray compound that is not attracted to magnets.

A compound can have different **properties,** depending on what state it is in. Think about one of the most common compounds we see every day: water. Each water molecule is made up of two atoms of hydrogen and one atom of oxygen.

We are all familiar with the three different states of water. We use liquid water for washing, drinking, and cooking. Liquid water that falls as rain helps plants to grow. Solid water makes up ice cubes, which we put in drinks, and falls as snow in cold weather. If you have ever gone ice-skating, you know that frozen water can be quite hard. Water in a gaseous form is called water vapor. There is water vapor in the air we breathe. Water becomes water vapor when it boils in a tea kettle or evaporates from a puddle in the sunlight.

Water can exist as a liquid, a solid, and a gas. Can you name the three states of water in this picture?

When a compound changes its state, some of its physical properties change, but the substance itself does not change. When liquid water freezes, it becomes a solid, but it is still water. Each water molecule is still made up of two hydrogen atoms and one oxygen atom.

However, some changes that compounds undergo actually change the substance of the compound. These are called chemical changes. In a chemical change the atoms in a compound's molecules break apart and combine again in new ways.

Burning is one of the most dramatic examples of a chemical change. Think of the wax in a candle. The wax is made up of molecules that contain carbon and hydrogen atoms. When the candle's wick is lit, wax is drawn up the wick and burns. The carbon and hydrogen atoms in the wax molecules separate and combine with oxygen in the air. This produces carbon dioxide gas and water vapor. A lot of energy is also released, which is why fire gives off light and heat.

Burning is one of the most dramatic examples of a chemical change.

This photograph of the Milky Way in the summer was taken from Mount Graham, Arizona.

Our Universe

From burning candles to freezing, melting, condensing, and evaporating water, understanding how elements interact helps us understand the world around us. The interaction of elements is not only important for understanding life on Earth but also for understanding how the universe works.

The universe is made up of everything that exists, including all the planets, stars, distant galaxies, and space dust. Everything in the universe is made of matter.

There are many theories as to how the universe came to be. Because it happened so long ago–some scientists believe between 10 billion and 20 billion years ago–there are very few clues that can be studied. However, scientists have observed that the universe seems to be expanding, leading them to believe that it was smaller at one point in time.

Some believe that it took 300,000 years from the beginning of the universe for the first atoms to form. They believe electrons came together with protons and neutrons to form hydrogen and helium, two of the simplest elements.

Within the universe are many galaxies, stars, and planets. All of these bodies are made of elements such as hydrogen, helium, and iron. How they have interacted with each other is very important in the formation of the universe as we know it.

Galaxies are clusters of stars, dust, and gas that are attracted to each other by gravity. The planet Earth and the rest of our solar system are a small part of the Milky Way galaxy. The Milky Way is shaped like a spiral with a round ball at the center. This ball is actually a compact clump of millions of stars. Our solar system, embedded in one of the spiral arms, consists of one star (the sun), nine planets with their moons, asteroids, comets, and space dust.

As suggested by its spiral shape, the Milky Way galaxy spins around in space.

The gravity of a black hole pulls gas from
the atmosphere of a blue giant star.

There are millions of stars in our galaxy. Some of them
we can see with the naked eye. Some can be seen only with
powerful telescopes. People used to think that the stars were
large balls of fire, or solid balls of burning material. We now
know that this is not true.

Stars are actually huge balls of gas that give off light, heat,
and other types of energy. All of this energy is produced by a
type of reaction called nuclear **fusion.** In nuclear fusion, two or
more atoms fuse together to make one larger atom.

This is different from a chemical reaction. Chemical
reactions produce new compounds, while fusion reactions
actually produce new elements.

Because the center of a star is very hot, its atoms move quickly. The center of a star is also very dense, so atoms often crash into each other. On Earth, atoms are repelled by each other. But in the center of a star, particles move so quickly and are so densely packed that they can strike each other at incredible speeds. When two hydrogen atoms strike each other, they can fuse together to form helium. This reaction releases a large amount of energy.

The temperature in a star must rise to about 10 million degrees Celsius (about 18 million degrees Fahrenheit) for nuclear fusion to occur. Once started, a star will change hydrogen into helium until there is no more hydrogen.

Stars can shine for billions of years, but all stars run out of hydrogen. When this happens, the star cools down and expands. At this stage, many stars turn into red giants. Some stars then collapse and turn into white dwarfs, which are as small as planets. Once white dwarfs have completely cooled, they become dark matter sometimes called black dwarf stars.

Some huge stars collapse in on themselves and form black holes. Very little is known about them. Scientists do know that black holes contain large amounts of matter and strong gravity.

Scientists think the core of the sun looks like this.

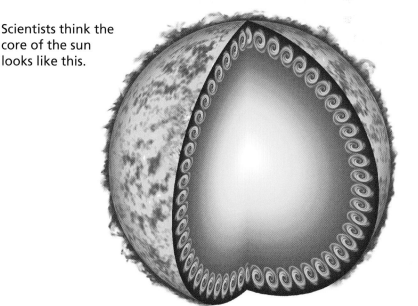

When you look up at the night sky, all the stars look basically alike, although you may notice that some are a bit brighter than others. If you observed the stars through a very powerful telescope, you would see that there are actually many different types of stars. They differ in color and size.

The color of a star indicates how hot it is. The hottest stars are either bluish-white or white. Other stars can be yellow, orange-white, or red.

Very bright stars are very heavy. Their great weight puts a lot of pressure on the material at the center of the star. This speeds up the fusion reaction, releasing more energy and making the star brighter. Very heavy stars do not last long, because they use up their hydrogen more quickly than lighter stars.

Although our sun is about one million times the volume of Earth, it is only a medium-sized star. Many stars are far larger. The size of stars has to do with the amount of matter that they contain. It also depends on the stage of life the star is in.

For example, Betelgeuse (pronounced *beetle-juice*) is one of the brightest stars in the sky. It is a red super-giant that makes the shoulder of the constellation Orion. Betelgeuse is more than 1,000 times the diameter of our sun.

On the other hand, there are stars that are much smaller than our sun. White dwarfs can be as small as Earth!

At the center of this reddish gas cloud is a white dwarf star.

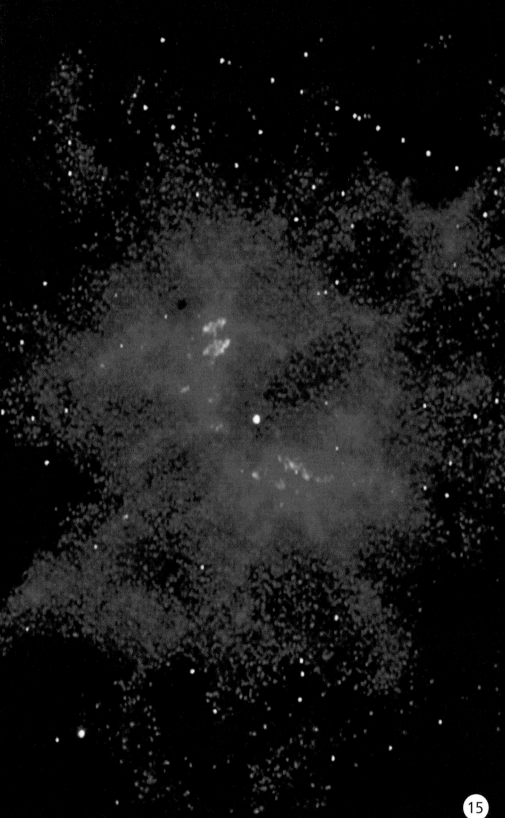

Our Solar System

The solar system we live in was also formed about 4.6 billion years ago. Just like the universe, our solar system is so old that it is hard for an **astronomer** studying it to know exactly how it was formed. There are many hypotheses. One hypothesis states that as the sun began to take shape at the center of a cloud of dust and gas, the rest of the matter formed a very thin disk around it. Gradually, the disk cooled and bits of matter clumped together. First, the **metallic** elements and rock condensed out of the cloudy disk, followed by ice. These clumps of matter formed the planets and moons of our solar system, as well as smaller bodies called asteroids and meteoroids.

Our solar system contains nine planets. The four that are closest to the sun are Mercury, Venus, Earth, and Mars. They are called the terrestrial planets. These planets are relatively close together and have many similar characteristics. Although scientists don't know exactly what the interiors of these planets are like, they can make logical guesses.

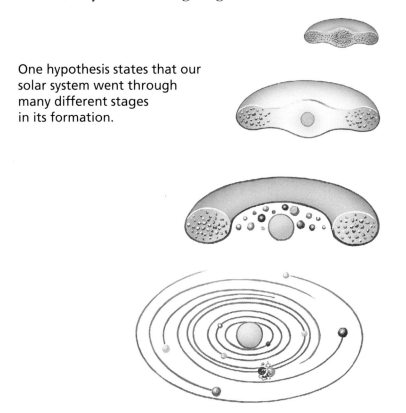

One hypothesis states that our solar system went through many different stages in its formation.

Clues from the planets' surfaces indicate that they probably have a thin crust on top of a thicker layer called the mantle. The planets' masses hint that they probably have dense cores made of iron. All of these planets, except Mercury, have atmospheres made of gases.

The next four planets are larger and farther apart. Jupiter, Saturn, Uranus, and Neptune are called gaseous planets, or gas giants. These planets are extremely large, and they have no solid surface. Instead, they are huge balls of gas. Some of them may have solid cores. Scientists believe that Jupiter's core may be made of solid hydrogen. On Earth, hydrogen is a gas. But Jupiter's mass is very great, producing very high pressures at its core. The pressure is so high that it compresses hydrogen gas into a solid.

Pluto, the planet farthest from the sun, is not like the terrestrial planets or the gaseous planets. It is so cold that it is covered in ice made of nitrogen and carbon monoxide. These substances are gases on Earth.

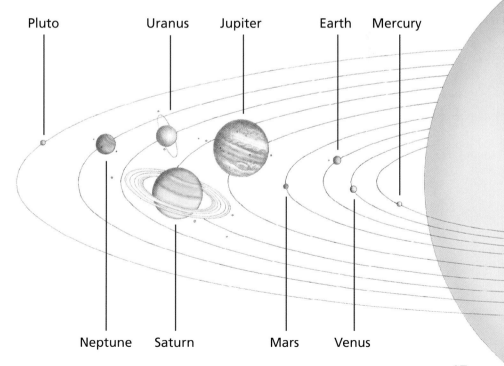

Pluto   Uranus   Jupiter   Earth   Mercury

Neptune   Saturn   Mars   Venus

Just the Right Elements for Life

As far as we know, Earth is a unique planet. It has just the right combination of elements to make it hospitable for living things. Earth appears to be the only planet in our solar system that can support life at this time.

For example, Venus and Earth are nearly identical in size, and they are both rocky planets. Until not long ago, many people thought that life probably existed on Venus. They pictured tropical forests covering the planet's surface. However, they were wrong.

The surface of Venus can reach about 462°C, or 864°F. The atmosphere is made up mostly of carbon dioxide, the compound that plants use to survive on Earth. However, carbon dioxide is poisonous to humans. The dense clouds that cover the planet contain drops of sulfuric acid, a mixture of the elements hydrogen and sulfur. Sulfuric acid is harmful to living things.

In addition to these **characteristics,** there is one more that prevents life on Venus. This is the lack of water on the planet. Earth is largely covered in water, a compound that is needed by all living things. Venus, on the other hand, is closer to the sun and therefore hotter than Earth. Water would evaporate into the atmosphere. **Radiation** from the sun would destroy the water molecules by breaking them into separate atoms.

Earth is the only planet that we know of that can sustain life.

A diamond and the graphite in a pencil are both made of pure carbon.

Another important factor for life on Earth is the element carbon. It is the sixth most common element in the universe, and it forms millions of compounds. Coal, oil, and natural gas are compounds of carbon. When combined with hydrogen and oxygen, carbon can form sugar, starch, and paper. It combines with elements such as nitrogen, phosphorous, and sulfur to make hair and muscle. In fact, all plant and animal cells are based on carbon.

Pure carbon on its own can take on a number of different forms too. Examples of pure carbon are diamonds, charcoal, and graphite. How does pure carbon take so many different forms? The answer lies in how the atoms of carbon bond together. For example, in diamonds the carbon atoms form a lattice structure that is very strong and allows light to pass through. In graphite, most often used to make pencils, the atoms are bonded together in sheets that can slide against each other.

Charcoal is also pure carbon.

Matter makes up everything.

Matter Is All Around Us

Matter makes up everything in the universe. Elements such as hydrogen and carbon consist of atoms with a certain number of protons, electrons, and neutrons. Scientists are not sure how all this matter formed, but it is a question they continue to try to answer. Somehow, bits of matter came together to form galaxies full of stars and planets, including our sun and the planets in our solar system. Matter also came together in very complicated ways to form life on Earth.

Atoms come together in many different ways to form elements that make up the matter around us. They are the building blocks of all things.

Scientists learn new things about the interaction of elements in our universe every day. Perhaps in the future, they will find new elements and new ways that they have come together.

Now Try This

Reactions

Here is an easy experiment that you can do at home or in class.

How can scientists tell that elements or compounds are reacting with each other to make new kinds of matter? Often they look for visible signs such as a change in color or the production of bubbles. The release of light or heat is another sign of a reaction. In this experiment we will mix two common substances and observe what happens.

What You Will Need
safety goggles
vinegar
teaspoon
tablespoon
baking soda
small bottle
balloon
funnel

1. Put on your safety goggles.
2. Pour a few teaspoons of vinegar into the bottle.
3. Using the funnel, pour a tablespoon of baking soda into the balloon.
4. Being careful not to pour the baking soda into the bottle, fit the balloon opening over the neck of the bottle.
5. Lift the balloon and let the baking soda fall into the vinegar.

What did you observe? What seemed to be happening in the bottle? What happened to the balloon? Do you think that different forms of matter were being made?

The acetic acid in the vinegar reacts with the sodium bicarbonate (baking soda) to form carbonic acid. Carbonic acid is unstable and decomposes into water and carbon dioxide, which is the gas that is released. Sodium acetate and water are left in the bottle.

Glossary

astronomer *n.* an expert in astronomy, the science that deals with the sun, moon, planets, stars, etc.

characteristics *n.* qualities that distinguish one person or thing from others.

elements *n.* the basic substances from which all things are made.

fusion *n.* the combining of two or more atomic nuclei to produce a nucleus of greater mass.

metallic *adj.* containing or consisting of metal.

properties *n.* qualities or powers belonging specially to something.

radiation *n.* particles or electromagnetic waves emitted by the atoms and molecules of a radioactive substance as a result of atomic decay.

Reader Response

1. What is the main idea of this book? Use a chart like the one below to write down the main idea and three supporting details.

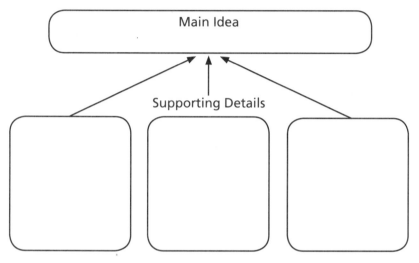

2. How are compounds different from elements? If you are not sure, which pages could you reread to find out?

3. Which two words listed in the Glossary are synonyms?

4. Based on the information in this book, do you think other planets that can sustain life exist in the universe? Explain your answer.

Science

Suggested levels for Guided Reading, DRA™, Lexile,® and Reading Recovery™ are provided in the Pearson Scott Foresman Leveling Guide.

Genre	Comprehension Skills and Strategy	Text Features
Expository nonfiction	• Main Idea • Cause and Effect • Monitor and Fix Up	• Diagrams • Captions • Labels • Glossary

Scott Foresman Reading Street 6.2.1

scottforesman.com

ISBN 0-328-13609-3

90000

9 780328 136094

Vocabulary

astronomer

characteristics

elements

fusion

metallic

properties

radiation

Word count: 2,755

Note: The total word count includes words in the running text and headings only. Numerals and words in chapter titles, captions, labels, diagrams, charts, graphs, sidebars, and extra features are not included.

Suggested levels for Guided Reading, DRA™, Lexile,® and Reading Recovery™ are provided in the Pearson Scott Foresman Leveling Guide.

Science

Genre	Comprehension Skills and Strategy	Text Features
Expository nonfiction	• Main Idea • Cause and Effect • Monitor and Fix Up	• Diagrams • Captions • Labels • Glossary

Scott Foresman Reading Street 6.2.1

PEARSON

Scott
Foresman

scottforesman.com

ISBN 0-328-13609-3

90000

9 780328 136094

Vocabulary

astronomer

characteristics

elements

fusion

metallic

properties

radiation

Word count: 2,755

Photo locators denoted as follows: Top (T), Center (C), Bottom (B), Left (L), Right (R), Background (Bkgd)

Opener: ©DK Images; 1 ©DK Images; 3 Getty Images; 4 ©DK Images; 5 PhotoEdit; 6 PhotoEdit; 7 NASA; 8 PhotoEdit; 9 ©DK Images; 10 ©DK Images; 11 ©DK Images; 12 ©DK Images; 13 ©DK Images; 15 ©DK Images; 16 PhotoLibrary, Comstock, ©DK Images; 17 ©DK Images; 18 Fundamental; 19 Aurora Photos; 20 ©DK Images, Getty Images; 21 NASA; 23 ©DK Images

ISBN: 0-328-13609-3

7 8 9 10 V0G1 14 13 12 11 10 09 08

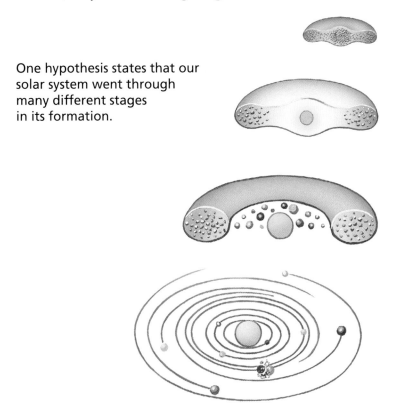

ISBN: 0-328-13609-3

7 8 9 10 V0G1 14 13 12 11 10 09 08

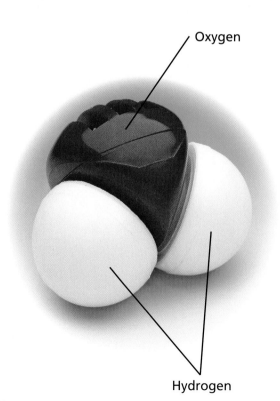

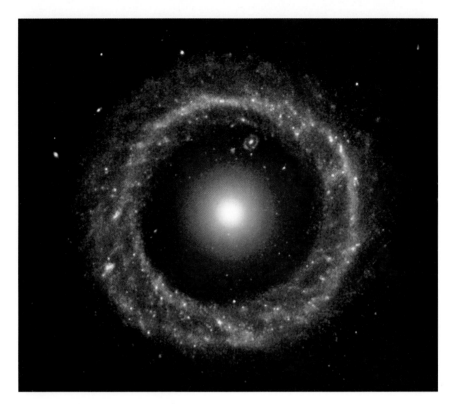

Vocabulary

astronomer

characteristics

elements

fusion

metallic

properties

radiation

Word count: 2,755

Note: The total word count includes words in the running text and headings only. Numerals and words in chapter titles, captions, labels, diagrams, charts, graphs, sidebars, and extra features are not included.

Vocabulary

astronomer

characteristics

elements

fusion

metallic

properties

radiation

Word count: 2,755

Every effort has been made to secure permission and provide appropriate credit for photographic material. The publisher deeply regrets any omission and pledges to correct errors called to its attention in subsequent editions.

Unless otherwise acknowledged, all photographs are the property of Scott Foresman, a division of Pearson Education.

Photo locators denoted as follows: Top (T), Center (C), Bottom (B), Left (L), Right (R), Background (Bkgd)

Opener: ©DK Images; 1 ©DK Images; 3 Getty Images; 4 ©DK Images; 5 PhotoEdit; 6 PhotoEdit; 7 NASA; 8 PhotoEdit; 9 ©DK Images; 10 ©DK Images; 11 ©DK Images; 12 ©DK Images; 13 ©DK Images; 15 ©DK Images; 16 PhotoLibrary, Comstock, ©DK Images; 17 ©DK Images; 18 Fundamental; 19 Aurora Photos; 20 ©DK Images, Getty Images; 21 NASA; 23 ©DK Images

ISBN: 0-328-13609-3

7 8 9 10 V0G1 14 13 12 11 10 09 08

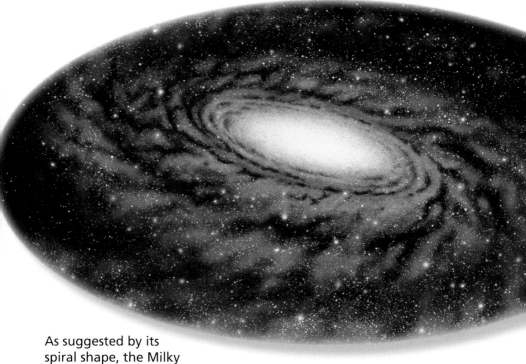

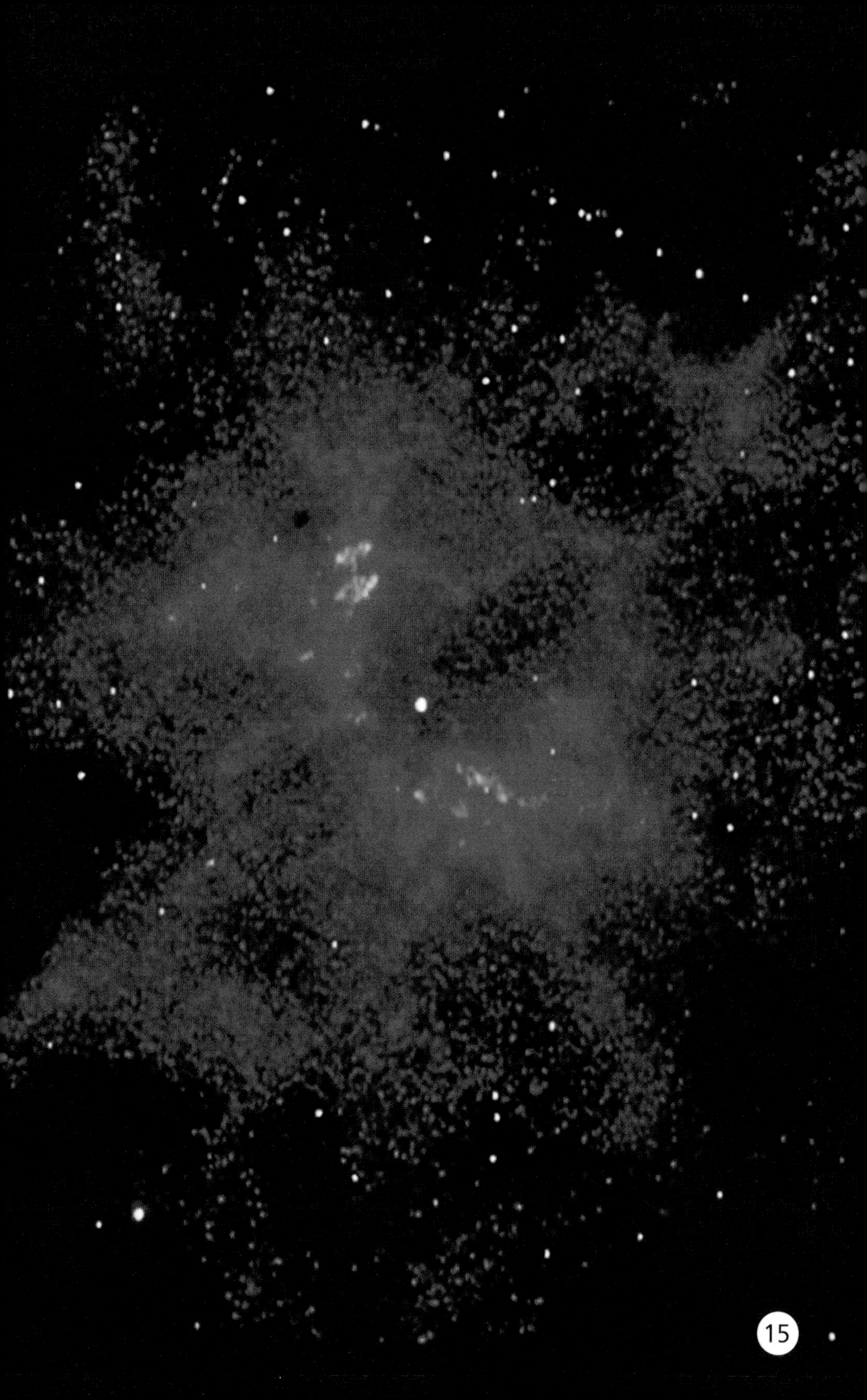